102 Simple English Conversation Dialogues For Beginners in American English: Gain Confidence and Improve your Spoken English

Jackie Bolen

www.eslspeaking.org

Copyright © 2021 by Jackie Bolen

All rights reserved. No part of this publication may be reproduced, distributed, or transmitted in any form or by any means, including photocopying, recording or other electronic or mechanical means without the prior written permission of the publisher, except in the case of brief quotations in critical reviews and certain other non-commercial uses permitted by copyright law. For permission requests, write to the publisher/author at the following address: Jackie Bolen: jb.business.online@gmail.com.

Table of Contents

About the Author: Jackie Bolen...6
Introduction...7
The Four-Step Reading Process..8
#1: Taking the Bus...9
#2: Getting Information from the Bus Driver...11
#3: Running Late..12
#4: Bob is Very Late..14
#5: The Ice Cream Shop...15
#6: Checking in at the Airport...16
#7: Talking to a Customer Service Agent...17
#8: Asking for directions..19
#9: Confused about Where the Store Is..20
#10: Deciding How to Get Somewhere...21
#11: Beach Day Tomorrow..22
#12: Traffic Jam...23
#13: Stuck in a Traffic Jam..24
#14: At the Market..25
#15: Shopping Plan...27
#16: Buying Clothes..29
#17: Window-Shopping..31
#18: Talking to a Delivery Driver...32
#19: Talking to a Clerk...33
#20: Buying a New Computer...35
#21: Talking about the News...37
#22: The Superbowl..38
#23: Talking about Upcoming Weekend Plans.....................................40
#24: Weekend Plans..41
#25: Talking about the Previous Weekend...42
#26: A Fun Weekend...43
#27: Playing Tennis...44
#28: Keep Playing?..45
#29: Watching a Baseball Game...46
#30: What to Eat at the Baseball Game..47
#31: Chit Chat..49
#32: Chatting at Lunch...51
#33: Talking about What to Eat at Home...52
#34: Deciding What to Cook...54
#35: Talking about What to Eat at a Restaurant...................................56
#36: A Big Restaurant Menu...58
#37: Doing Chores...59
#38: How to Split Chores...61
#39: Talking about Holidays...63
#40: Vacation Plans...64
#41: Talking about a New Neighbor..65

3

#42: Another New Neighbor 66
#43: At the Movie Theater 67
#44: Getting Snacks at the Movie Theater 68
#45: At the Cafe 69
#46: Deciding What to Order 70
#47: Making a Special Order at a Restaurant 72
#48: Gluten-Free Options 73
#49: A Suspicious Person 74
#50: The New Guy 76
#51: Talking About an Accident 78
#52: A Recent Accident 80
#53: Talking about Hobbies 82
#54: Talking about Hiking 84
#55: Talking about Pets 86
#56: A New Dog 87
#57: Talking About the Weather 88
#58: A Heatwave 90
#59: Talking About a New Phone 92
#60: Bob's New Phone 94
#61: Talking About an Upcoming Wedding 96
#62: Going to a Wedding 98
#63: Talking About Health Problems 100
#64: Talking about Health Problems 102
#65: Talking About a Teacher 103
#66: The English Teacher 105
#67: Talking about Getting to School 106
#68: Traffic 108
#69: Help With Moving 110
#70: Help with an Assignment 111
#71: Bumping into Someone 112
#72: Turn Up the Music 114
#73: The Sleepover 116
#74: A Ride to the Airport 118
#75: Catching a Movie 120
#76: Some Sad News 122
#77: A Terrible Cold 123
#78: Signing up for a Class 125
#79: At the Library 127
#80: At the Coffee Shop 129
#81: At the Dentist 131
#82: Getting a Beer After Work 133
#83: Burgers for Dinner 134
#84: Another Date 136
#85: Bad Weather for the Weekend 138
#86: New Shoes 140
#87: Getting a Refund 142
#88: Ordering a Cake 144

#89: Taking a Taxi...146
#90: A Noisy Hotel Room..148
#91: Making an Appointment 149
#92: Talking to the Doctor..151
#93: More Ketchup, Please 153
#94: No Mayo, Please 155
#95: A Phone Problem..156
#96: Cancelling an Appointment 158
#97: Ordering Sushi..160
#98: Leaving a Message?...162
#99: Reporting an Accident..164
#100: A Hangover...166
#101: Refrigerator Problems...167
#102: A Missing Package...169
Before You Go..171

About the Author: Jackie Bolen

I taught English in South Korea for 10 years to every level and type of student. I've taught every age from kindergarten kids to adults. These days, I'm teaching in Vancouver, Canada

I hold a Master of Arts in Psychology. During my time in Korea I successfully completed the CELTA and DELTA teacher certification programs. With the combination of almost ten years teaching ESL/EFL learners of all ages and levels, and the more formal teaching qualifications I've obtained, I have a solid foundation on which to offer advice to English learners.

Please send me an email with any questions or feedback.

YouTube: www.youtube.com/c/jackiebolen

Pinterest: www.pinterest.com/eslspeaking

ESL Speaking: www.eslspeaking.org

Email: jb.business.online@gmail.com

You might also be interested in these books (by Jackie Bolen):

- 1001 English Expressions and Phrases

- The Big Book of Phrasal Verbs in Use

- English Grammar Workbook for Beginners

Please join my email list. You'll get a helpful email, related to learning English delivered to your inbox every week: www.eslspeaking.org/learn-english.

Introduction

Welcome to this book designed to help you expand your knowledge of American English. My goal is to help you speak and write more fluently.

Let's face it, English can be difficult to master, even for the best students. In this book, you'll find 102 American English dialogues that are ideal for beginners.

The best way to learn new vocabulary is in context.

To get the most bang for your buck, be sure to do the following:

- Review frequently.

- Try to use some of the phrases and expressions in real life.

- Don't be nervous about making mistakes. That's how you'll get better at English!

- Consider studying with a friend so you can help each other stay motivated.

- Use a notebook and write down new words, idioms, expressions, etc. that you run across. Review frequently so that they stay fresh in your mind.

- Be sure to answer the questions at the end of each dialogue. I recommend trying to do this from memory. No peeking!

- I recommend doing one dialogue a day. This will be more beneficial than finishing the entire book in a week or two.

The Four-Step Reading Process

Here's what I recommend doing for each of the dialogues in order to get the most benefit from them.

#1: Read the Introduction

Be sure to read the introduction at the start of each dialogue. This helps to set the context and will make what you're reading more memorable. Think about if you've experienced a similar situation before.

#2: Read the Conversation Quickly

Read the whole conversation through quickly, without stopping to look up words or phrases. If you don't know something, make your best guess as to what it is. Think about the overall meaning and what's happening.

#3: Read for Detail

Go back and read the conversation one more time. Look up words that you don't know and write them down in a notebook. If you don't understand everything, read the dialogue again.

#4: Read the Questions and Answer Them

There are three questions at the end of each dialogue. Read them carefully and see if you can answer them from memory. If you can't, go back and find the answer in the dialogue. Check your answers.

#1: Taking the Bus

Ted and Chris are trying to figure out how to get to the airport from downtown.

Ted: How are we going to get to the airport tomorrow?

Chris: Isn't there a bus that goes there?

Ted: Probably. Do you know which one?

Chris: I think number seven is the airport bus but let's check online and see.

Ted: Sure, I have my computer right here.

Chris: Perfect.

Ted: Okay. It is the number seven. It leaves every twenty minutes and the stop is just a few minutes away from here. Let's try to get the 1:20? That leaves us plenty of time.

Chris: Sounds like a plan.

Check Your Understanding

1. Where are they going?

2. How often does the airport bus run?

3. Where is the bus stop?

Answers

1. They are going to the airport.

2. The bus runs every twenty minutes.

3. The bus stop is only a few minutes away.

#2: Getting Information from the Bus Driver

Johnny wants to find out some information from the bus driver.

Johnny: Does this bus go downtown?

Bus Driver: No, you'll need to take the number six instead.

Johnny: Oh, okay. Can I catch it at this bus stop?

Bus Driver: You'll want to cross the street and take the bus in the other direction.

Johnny: Okay. Great. Thank you. Oh, do you know how often it runs?

Bus Driver: I don't know exactly but there are a lot of them. During rush hour, maybe every 10 minutes.

Check Your Understanding

1. Where does Johnny want to go?
2. Which bus goes downtown?
3. How often does the bus run at 2:00 in the afternoon?

Answers

1. He wants to go downtown.
2. The #6 bus goes downtown.
3. Not enough information. We only know about rush hour.

#3: Running Late

Zeke wants to let Sid know that he is running late.

Zeke: Sid. Hi. So sorry but I'm going to be late for dinner.

Sid: Oh, okay. What time do you think you'll get here?

Zeke: By 7:00 at the latest, I think. There was an accident ahead of me on the highway.

Sid: Oh no! Is it cleared?

Zeke: It will be soon I think. It looks like the police are finishing up now and traffic is moving slowly.

Sid: Sure. See you when you get here. No rush. I'll just have a glass of wine and wait.

Zeke: Thanks for understanding. I appreciate it.

Check Your Understanding

1. What time was their dinner plan?

2. Who is going to be late?

3. What will Sid do while he waits?

Answers

1. Their dinner meeting time was before 7:00.

2. Zeke is going to be late.

3. He's going to have a glass of wine.

#4: Bob is Very Late

Tammy is annoyed at Bob for being late again.

Tammy: Bob! Where are you? I'm already here. We were supposed to meet at 7:00.

Bob: I'm so sorry. I lost track of time.

Tammy: Have you even left your house yet?

Bob: No. But I can leave in a minute. I'm ready to go now.

Tammy: Don't bother Bob. By the time you get here, you'll be over an hour late.

Bob: Why don't we reschedule?

Tammy: No, thank you. This is the third time this has happened.

Check Your Understanding

1. What time were they supposed to meet?
2. How late is Bob going to be?
3. Did they make another plan?

Answers

1. They were supposed to meet at 7:00.
2. He'll be more than one hour late.
3. No, Tammy doesn't want to make another plan because this is the third time Bob is late.

#5: The Ice Cream Shop

Mandy and Todd are deciding what kind of ice cream to get.

Mandy: There are so many choices here!

Todd: I know, that's why I like to come here. What are you thinking about?

Mandy: I know it's boring but I usually just get the same thing every time. I go for one scoop of cookies & cream and one scoop rainbow sherbet.

Todd: Those are classics for sure! Can't go wrong with them.

Mandy: What do you like?

Todd: I like to mix it up and get something different every time. I think I'll go for the salted caramel.

Check your Understanding

1. Who usually gets the same thing every time?
2. What is Todd going to get?
3. Why does Todd go to that ice cream shop?

Answers

1. Mandy usually get the same thing each time.
2. He's going to get salted caramel.
3. He goes there because there are so many choices.

#6: Checking in at the Airport

Bob and Gary are at the airport talking about where to check in for their flight.

Bob: Do you know where the check-in counter is?

Gary: I'm not sure. Let's check the board.

Bob: I see it. Flight 877. Counter 3.

Gary: Which way is that? This place is so big! I don't want to start walking in the wrong direction.

Bob: Hmm. Oh. There's 7 and 8 and 9. It must be the other way.

Gary: Alright. Let's go! We're pretty late. Boarding is starting soon! Let's walk quickly.

Check Your Understanding

1. Which check-in counter do they have to go to?
2. How big is the airport?
3. Are they early?

Answers

1. They have to go to counter 3.
2. The airport is very big. There are at least nine check-in counters.
3. No, they don't have much time.

#7: Talking to a Customer Service Agent

Tim is talking with a customer service agent at the airport.

Customer Service Agent: Where are you headed?

Tim: I'm going to Tokyo.

Customer Service Agent: Okay. Can I see your passport, please?

Tim: Sure.

Customer Service Agent: Would you like a window or aisle seat?

Tim: Aisle seat, please.

Customer Service Agent: Sure. How many bags?

Tim: Just one.

Customer Service Agent: Okay. Put it on the belt and here are your tickets. The boarding time is 7:35. Have a good flight.

Tim: Thank you.

Check Your Understanding

1. How many bags does Tim have?

2. Where is Tim going?

3. Where does Tim want to sit?

Answers

1. Tim has one bag.

2. He's going to Tokyo

3. He wants an aisle seat.

#8: Asking for directions

Jim is lost and needs directions.

Jim: Excuse me. Do you know where Luigi's restaurant is?

Matt: I've never heard of it. What's the address?

Jim: It's on the corner of 10th Avenue and 7th Street.

Matt: Oh, it must be right next to the Starbucks. You're pretty close. Go down this street for about 2 blocks and then you'll see it on your left.

Jim: Thanks for your help!

Matt: No problem at all.

Check Your Understanding

1. Where is Jim going?
2. What is the restaurant next to?
3. How far away is the restaurant?

Answers

1. He's going to Luigi's.
2. The restaurant is next to a *Starbucks*.
3. The restaurant is two blocks away.

#9: Confused about Where the Store Is

Mary is on the phone with a store employee to ask for directions.

Mary: Hi, I'm trying to get to your store but I'm a bit confused.

Clerk: Okay. Where are you now?

Mary: I came to the correct address on Google Maps but I don't see your place.

Clerk: Sure. We're actually inside the grocery store. Do you see it?

Mary: Yes, I'm right in front of it.

Clerk: Come into the store and we're at the back, on the left.

Mary: Perfect. Thank you.

Check Your Understanding

1. Why is Mary calling the store?
2. Why can't Mary find the store?
3. Is the stop at the front or back of the grocery store?

Answers

1. She's calling because she can't find the store.
2. She can't find the store because it's inside the grocery store.
3. The shop is at the back of the grocery store.

#10: Deciding How to Get Somewhere

Bob and Keith are talking about how to get downtown for a concert.

Keith: Where's the concert? And, it's at 8:30, right?

Bob: It's at The Orpheum, downtown. It starts at 9:00 actually.

Keith: Parking is so expensive downtown. What about taking the subway there instead of driving?

Bob: That's good for getting there but it stops running at 11:30 I think. We might have to take a taxi home.

Keith: That's fine with me. It'll be about $20 each.

Check Your Understanding

1. What time does the concert start?
2. How are they getting there? Why?
3. How are they getting home? Why?

Answers

1. The concert starts at 9:00.
2. They are taking the subway because parking is expensive.
3. They are taking a taxi home because it'll be too late to take the subway.

#11: Beach Day Tomorrow

Mary and Sarah are talking about going to the beach.

Mary: How are we going to get to the beach tomorrow?

Sarah: I don't mind driving.

Mary: Sure. But, won't it be so busy at 1:00 when we planned to go? We might not find a spot.

Sarah: You're right. That's when everyone is there. What about going later at around 4:00? We can catch the sunset.

Mary: Sure, that sounds good.

Check Your Understanding

1. What time are they going to the beach?
2. Why are they going later?
3. Who is driving?

Answers

1. They're going at 4:00.
2. They're going later because it might be difficult to find parking at 1:00.
3. Sarah is driving.

#12: Traffic Jam

Lucy and Warren are commuting to work together.

Lucy: I can't believe traffic is so bad!

Warren: I know. It's busier than normal. I wonder what's up.

Lucy: Maybe there's an accident. I'll check Google Maps and see what it says.

Warren: Sure.

Lucy: Oh no! There are two accidents up ahead. It'll take us another hour to get to work. We'll both be late for sure.

Warren: I don't want to rush. No sense getting into an accident.

Lucy: Let me text our bosses to let them know. You focus on driving.

Check Your Understanding

1. Who is driving?
2. Why are they going to be late?
3. Why is Lucy going to text her boss?

Answers

1. Warren is driving.
2. They are going to be late because there are two accidents.
3. She is going to text her boss to let her know she'll be late.

#13: Stuck in a Traffic Jam

Richard is stuck in a traffic jam and telling Linda that he'll be late for their appointment.

Richard: Linda? Hi. Sorry, I'm going to be late for coffee.

Linda: Oh no. What time will you be here?

Richard: It's hard to say. There's a lot of traffic. I'll be as fast as I can.

Linda: Okay. Keep me updated, please. I need to leave in about an hour to pick up my kids from school.

Richard: I didn't know you needed to leave at a specific time. I'll try to hurry. Sorry again.

Linda: Sure.

Check Your Understanding

1. Why is Richard going to be late?

2. What is Linda doing after she has coffee?

3. How long can Linda wait?

Answers

1. He's going to be late because there's a lot of traffic.

2. After coffee, Linda is going to pick up her kids from school.

3. She can only wait for an hour.

#14: At the Market

Kerry and Tracy are at the farmer's market.

Kerry: Look how nice these tomatoes are. Should we get some?

Tracy: Sure. Let's make bruschetta tonight for dinner.

Kerry: Perfect. Then we'll need some garlic and basil too. And fresh bread.

Tracy: Definitely. Let's get some fruit too for lunches. Maybe some peaches or grapes?

Kerry: Okay. I also want to check out those cookies and cakes over there.

Tracy: There are so many good things here! I'm happy we decided to come.

Kerry: Me too. Look! Homemade vegan samosas. Let's pick up a few of those for tomorrow.

Tracy: Perfect. I hope we have enough bags to carry all of this stuff!

Check Your Understanding

1. What are Tracy and Kerry making for dinner tonight?

2. Why are they getting fruit?

3. What kind of samosas are they buying?

Answers

1. They are going to make bruschetta for dinner.

2. They are getting fruit for their lunches.

3. They are buying vegan samosas.

#15: Shopping Plan

Harry and Mo are deciding on a shopping strategy at the supermarket.

Harry: What do you think? Should we divide and conquer or stick together this week?

Mo: How much stuff do we need to buy?

Harry: Not that much. Just fruit and vegetables, milk, bread and a couple of other things.

Mo: Why don't we stick together then. It won't take very long to get all this stuff.

Harry: Sure, but I get to push the cart, okay? It's my favourite!

Mo: Whatever you want! Here. You hold the list too and cross off the stuff as we buy it.

Harry: Okay. You're so bossy!

Check Your Understanding

1. Why are they doing the shopping together?

2. Who is pushing the cart?

3. Where are they shopping?

Answers

1. They are doing it together because they don't have many things to buy.

2. Harry is pushing the cart.

3. They are shopping at the supermarket.

#16: Buying Clothes

Ben is shopping with his dad for new clothes for school.

Terry: Okay. So what's on the list you and your mom made? Let's see: 2 pairs of pants, a couple of t-shirts, a hoodie and some running shoes?

Ben: Yes. I think that's it. Oh, maybe some socks and underwear. Mine are getting too small.

Terry: Sure, we'll buy four or five of each of those. Which store did you want to start at?

Ben: Uggghhh...I don't like shopping. Let's go to *Uniqlo* and we can hopefully find everything but the shoes there.

Terry: I don't like it either but let's work together to get this done as quickly as possible.

Ben: Sounds good to me.

Check Your Understanding

1. Do Ben and Terry like shopping?

2. How many pairs of pants are they buying?

3. Who needs new clothes? Why?

Answers

1. Ben and Terry do not like shopping.

2. They are buying two pairs of pants.

3. Ben needs new clothes for school.

#17: Window-Shopping

Tina and Mary are doing some window-shopping.

Tina: Ohhh...look at those nice sweaters. They're so beautiful.

Mary: Do you want to go in and check them out?

Tina: Hmmm. I said that I wouldn't spend any money today.

Mary: Come on, let's just go see. It can't hurt.

Tina: Okay, you're right. But don't let me get my credit card out!

Mary: I'll do my best but I make no promises. I know how crazy you get when you like something!

Tina: You know me so well.

Check Your Understanding

    1. Are Tina and Mary planning on spending money?

    2. What catches Tina's eye?

    3. If Tina buys something, how would she pay for it?

Answers

    1. No, they aren't planning on spending money.

    2. Tina sees a sweater that she likes.

    3. She would pay with a credit card.

#18: Talking to a Delivery Driver

Bob is trying to arrange his delivery.

Delivery driver: Hi, Bob?

Bob: Yes, that's me.

Delivery driver: I have a package for you. Are you home now?

Bob: No, I'm at work. Can you leave it at my back door?

Delivery driver: Sure, will do. I'll sign your name for it, okay?

Bob: That's fine. Thank you.

Check Your Understanding

1. Where is Bob right now?
2. Why is the delivery driver calling?
3. Where is the delivery driver going to leave the package?

Answers

1. Bob is at work.
2. The driver is calling because he has a package for Bob but he's not at home.
3. The driver is going to leave the package at the back door.

#19: Talking to a Clerk

Rose is trying to find a specific t-shirt.

Rose: Excuse me. I'm wondering if you have this t-shirt in a small?

Clerk: There are none on the shelf?

Rose: I looked through them all.

Clerk: Okay, let me check the computer. Hmmm...we don't have any at this store. But, there are lots in stock in Burnaby. Do you want to go there, or we can get them to ship one here.

Rose: When could I come back to get it?

Clerk: It would take two or three days. We can give you a call when it's here.

Rose: Okay. I think I'll just head over to Burnaby. Thank you.

Check Your Understanding

1. What size of shirt is Rose looking for?

2. Can she find the shirt at that store?

3. Where is Rose going to get the shirt?

Answers

1. Rose is looking for a small shirt.

2. No, they don't have that specific shirt there.

3. She will go to the Burnaby store to get the shirt.

#20: Buying a New Computer

Keith is shopping for a new computer.

Clerk: Do you need any help finding something?

Keith: I'm looking for a new laptop but I'm kind of overwhelmed with all the choices.

Clerk: Sure, I can help you out. What did you need it for?

Keith: Basic stuff. Watching Netflix. Online banking. Email and Facebook. That kind of stuff.

Clerk: Sure, we have some cheaper computers that'll be perfect for that. Don't waste your money on these high-end gaming computers.

Keith: That sounds great to me. I hate computer games.

Clerk: Okay. Let's take a look at some of them.

Check Your Understanding

1. Does Keith like to play computer games?

2. Is Keith going to buy a cheap or expensive computer?

3. Why does Keith feel overwhelmed?

Answers

1. Keith does not like computer games.

2. He is going to buy a cheaper computer.

3. He feels overwhelmed because there are so many choices at the store.

#21: Talking about the News

Tim and Mary are talking about what they saw on the news last night.

Tim: Did you hear about the big hurricane that hit South Carolina last night?

Mary: So crazy, right? I heard the winds were almost 200 km/h.

Tim: Of course the power went out but I hope everyone was prepared for it.

Mary: I think they get hurricanes there every year. They must know what to do, right?

Tim: I hope so. I haven't heard how many people died yet.

Mary: I hope it turns out okay for everyone.

Tim: Me too. I hate to see stuff like that on the news.

Check Your Understanding

1. What kind of natural disaster are they talking about?
2. Where was the hurricane? Is that where they're living?
3. How strong is the wind?

Answers

1. They are talking about a hurricane.
2. The hurricane was in South Carolina. They are not living there.
3. There are very, very strong winds.

#22: The Superbowl

Jody and Sam are talking about the Superbowl.

Jody: Did you see the big game last night?

Sam: Of course! Who didn't?

Jody: What did you think?

Sam: Well, it was an interesting game but the real star was the half-time show. I couldn't believe how well done it was. I even watched it again on *YouTube* this morning.

Jody: I have to admit. I don't like Maroon 5 so I skipped the show! I was way more interested in the game. I made all kinds of snacks during halftime instead.

Sam: Check it out. Even if you don't like them, I think you'll enjoy the show.

Check Your Understanding

1. Who doesn't like Maroon 5?

2. What was Jody doing during the halftime show?

3. What was the "big game" the night before?

Answers

1. Jody doesn't like Maroon 5.

2. Jody was making snacks during the halftime show.

3. The big game was the Superbowl.

#23: Talking about Upcoming Weekend Plans

Sammy and Allan are talking about their weekend plans.

Sammy: What are you up to this weekend?

Allan: Oh, not much. I might spend some time getting the garden ready. It's that time of year, right?

Sammy: It is for sure. The days are getting longer.

Allan: What are you up to?

Sammy: Oh, not much. Just hanging out with my boyfriend. We just moved in together so have all kinds of stuff to organize and tidy up.

Allan: Oh, that's exciting. When did that happen?

Sammy: Last weekend.

Check Your Understanding

1. When did Sammy move in with her boyfriend?
2. What is Allan going to do this weekend?
3. What is Sammy going to do this weekend?

Answers

1. They moved in together last weekend.
2. He is going to do some work in his garden.
3. She is going to hang out, organize, and tidy up.

#24: Weekend Plans

Jenny and Ted are making some plans for the weekend.

Jenny: Ted, let's hang out this weekend! It's been a while.

Ted: I know, right? We haven't hung out in months. I'd love to do something. What do you think?

Jenny: The weather is supposed to be nice on Saturday. What about going for a hike? And then we can grab something to eat after?

Ted: That's great. Let's go to Mount Seymour. I haven't been there in a long time.

Jenny: Perfect. I can drive. I'll pick you up at 1:00?

Ted: Okay. See you then! I'll bring snacks for us.

Jenny: Perfect.

Check Your Understanding

1. What are they going to do together?

2. Who is bringing snacks?

3. What are they doing after hiking?

Answers

1. They are planning on going hiking.

2. Ted is going to bring snacks.

3. They'll get something to eat after hiking.

#25: Talking about the Previous Weekend

Kim and Andy are talking about what they did on the weekend.

Andy: How was your weekend?

Kim: Ugghhh...boring. My son was sick so I had to stay home and look after him. I did clean out the garage though.

Andy: Is he okay now?

Kim: Yeah. He went to school today. It was just the weekend when the weather was so nice! How was yours?

Andy: Tough break! I did all kinds of stuff. I went for a bike ride and played soccer with some friends. Then we had some patio beers after the game.

Kim: That sounds amazing.

Check Your Understanding

1. Why did Kim stay home on the weekend?
2. Is Kim's son still sick?
3. Did Andy go outside on the weekend?

Answers

1. She stayed home because her son was sick.
2. No, he's fine now.
3. Yes, he went for a bike ride and played soccer.

#26: A Fun Weekend

Kara and Casey are talking about what they did on the weekend.

Kara: Hey Casey. Did you have a good weekend?

Casey: The best. How about you?

Kara: Same here. What did you do?

Casey: Well, the weather was great so I went to the beach all of Saturday and brought my paddleboard too. What did you get up to?

Kara: I went to the Sufjan Stevens concert. Amazing.

Casey: I heard about that but I couldn't get tickets in time. I'm happy you had a good time.

Check Your Understanding

1. What did Casey do on the weekend?
2. What did Kara do on the weekend?
3. How was the weather on Saturday?

Answers

1. She went to the beach.
2. She went to a concert.
3. The weather was nice on Saturday.

#27: Playing Tennis

Ted and Sam are making plans to play tennis.

Ted: Hey, do you want to play tennis on Sunday?

Sam: I'd love to. Where do you usually play?

Ted: At Gates Park. What about meeting there at 1:00?

Sam: That sounds perfect. I'll see you then.

Ted: Should we invite two more people or play singles?

Sam: Let's play singles. I need a good run.

Ted: Okay. I should get more exercise too!

Check Your Understanding

1. Where are they playing tennis?

2. How many people are playing?

3. When are they playing?

Answers

1. They are playing tennis at Gates Park.

2. Two people are playing.

3. They are playing on Sunday at 1:00.

#28: Keep Playing?

Yvonne and Warren are talking about whether to play another set.

Yvonne: Nice win! You played so well. Isn't that the first time you beat me?

Warren: I think it is. Are you up for another set?

Yvonne: Hmm, I have enough energy but what time is it?

Warren: 2:20.

Yvonne: Okay. I need to be home at 3:00 for when the kids get home from school. Let's play until 2:45. We can maybe get a few more games in.

Warren: Sure. I'll set an alarm on my phone for 2:45.

Check Your Understanding

1. Who usually wins?

2. Are they playing another set?

3. Why does Yvonne need to leave at 2:45?

Answers

1. Yvonne usually wins.

2. They are going to play another set but they might not finish.

3. She has to be there when her kids get home from school.

#29: Watching a Baseball Game

John and Mel are chatting during a baseball game.

John: Did you see that hit?

Mel: Wait. What happened? I was checking my emails!

John: They might show it on the screen again. Alex Garcia took a super low pitch and popped it right over the head of the second baseman.

Mel: Ahhh. I always miss the action.

John: Well, put your phone away my friend! Haha.

Mel: You're right. It's a terrible habit.

Check Your Understanding

1. Why didn't Mel see the hit?
2. What is Mel's terrible habit?
3. Who hit the ball?

Answers

1. He didn't see it because he was checking his emails.
2. His terrible habit is that he's always on his phone.
3. Alex Garcia hit the ball.

#30: What to Eat at the Baseball Game

Tommy and Alex are talking about snacks.

Tommy: Hey, I'm going to go the bathroom. Would you like me to grab you something?

Alex: Sure, I'd love another beer, please. Oh, and one of those big pretzels too. And a bottle of water. I'm so thirsty. Can you carry it all?

Tommy: No problem. They give you a box if you have lots of stuff.

Alex: Oh, let me grab you some money. Here's $20. I think that should be enough.

Tommy: I'll let you know. It should be good.

Alex: Awesome. Thank you.

Check Your Understanding

1. What does Alex want to eat and drink?

2. How much money did Alex give Tommy?

3. How can Tommy carry everything?

Answers

1. Alex wants a beer, pretzel and bottle of water.

2. He gave him $20.

3. He can use a box to carry everything.

#31: Chit Chat

Ted and Ethan are catching up after not seeing each other for a while.

Ted: Long time, no talk Ethan. What's up?

Ethan: I know, right? It's probably been at least six months.

Ted: Too long.

Ethan: Well, I just started a new job and it's going pretty well.

Ted: Oh wow. Congratulations.

Ethan: Yeah. It's worked out well. What's up with you?

Ted: Same old, same old. Work is super busy these days and they don't want to hire more people because of Covid.

Ethan: Sounds tough.

Ted: I'll survive. Just barely though.

Check Your Understanding

1. How long has it been since they talked?

2. Who just started a new job?

3. Why isn't Ted's company hiring new people?

Answers

1. It has been at least six months.

2. Ethan started a new job.

3. They aren't hiring because of Covid.

#32: Chatting at Lunch

Nathan and Ed are chatting over lunch at the office.

Nathan: I haven't seen you in a while. How's your family doing?

Ed: Oh, good. Alice just started playing soccer and Kenny is getting into Scouts.

Nathan: Oh that sounds good. They grow up so fast, right?

Ed: They sure do. How are you doing?

Nathan: Not much new here. My girlfriend and I are talking about moving in together so that's kind of a big thing.

Ed: Nice! That's a big thing for sure.

Check Your Understanding

1. What is Nathan's big news?
2. What activities do the kids do?
3. Do Nathan and Ed see each other regularly?

Answers

1. Nathan and his girlfriend are considering moving in together.
2. They play soccer and do Scouts.
3. No, they don't.

#33: Talking about What to Eat at Home

Gary and Sam are talking about what to cook for dinner.

Gary: What should we make for dinner?

Sam: Uggghhhh...I don't feel like cooking. Let's go out.

Gary: No. We just spent $200 on groceries yesterday! Let's cook something. Let's see. We have so many veggies and some tofu. How about a tofu stir-fry?

Sam: Okay. I could do that. What kind of sauce?

Gary: Let's make some homemade sweet and sour sauce. It's easy to do I think.

Sam: All right. I'll put the rice on and start with the vegetables. You can do the sauce.

Gary: Sure thing. Let's get this done!

Check Your Understanding

1. Why does Sam want to eat out?

2. What are they going to make for dinner?

3. Who's taking care of the rice and vegetables?

Answers

1. He wants to eat out because he doesn't feel like cooking.

2. They are going to make a tofu stir-fry with sweet and sour sauce.

3. Sam is going to take care of the rice and vegetables.

#34: Deciding What to Cook

Stephen and Amar are talking about what to cook.

Stephen: I always hate the day before we go grocery shopping. It feels like we have nothing to eat.

Amar: Well, let's take a look! I'm sure we can figure something out.

Stephen: Okay. We have some lettuce that needs to be eaten, a tomato and some carrots. We can start with a salad and I'll make some homemade dressing.

Amar: Hmmm...and we have some hummus. We can have that with some crackers.

Stephen: Sure. Let's break open that jar of homemade pickles too!

Amar: Perfect. This sounds like a decent dinner!

Check Your Understanding

1. When are they doing grocery shopping?

2. Why are they going to have salad?

3. What are they eating the hummus with?

Answers

1. They are going shopping the next day.

2. They are going to have salad because they need to eat the lettuce.

3. They are going to eat it with some crackers.

#35: Talking about What to Eat at a Restaurant

Sharon and Mel are talking about what to eat.

Sharon: What are you going to get?

Mel: I'm trying to decide between the veggie burger or the Thai salad. What about you?

Sharon: Both of those sound great, especially the salad. I think I'm going to go for the pizza but I don't know what kind yet.

Mel: Pizza. Yum! How about splitting a meat lover's pizza and the salad?

Sharon: That sounds like such a good plan.

Mel: Let's do it.

Check Your Understanding

1. Are they each going to get their own meal?

2. What kind of pizza are they getting?

3. What kind of salad are they getting?

Answers

1. No, they are going to share two things.

2. They are getting a meat lover's pizza.

3. They are getting a Thai salad.

#36: A Big Restaurant Menu

Peter and Ilene are talking about the menu at a restaurant.

Peter: This menu is huge! I feel a bit overwhelmed.

Ilene: Me too. But their specialty is burgers so I think I'm going to stick with that.

Peter: That's a good idea. Let's see.

Ilene: Chicken, beef, veggie, fish...still so many options!

Peter: I'm going to go for a veggie burger. I'm trying to eat healthier these days but of course, I'm going to get fries with it.

Ilene: A chicken burger for me I think! The Hawaiian with grilled pineapple sounds delicious.

Check Your Understanding

1. What is the specialty at that restaurant?
2. What kind of burger is Peter getting? Why?
3. What kind of burger is Ilene getting?

Answers

1. The restaurant specializes in burgers.
2. He's getting a veggie burger because he wants to eat healthier.
3. She's getting a Hawaiian chicken burger.

#37: Doing Chores

Tim and Emily are talking about a plan for cleaning their house.

Tim: Let's get this place cleaned up! It's so messy and dirty.

Emily: I know. I hate it. Okay, why don't we put all the stuff away first? Then it'll be easier to clean.

Tim: Good plan. After that, why don't I tackle the bathrooms and you can do the floors.

Emily: Sure. I'll throw a load of laundry in first though.

Tim: Okay. Then we can tackle the dusting and clean up the kitchen and whatever else there is to do.

Emily: Uggghhh...this is going to take us so long!

Check Your Understanding

1. What task are they doing first?

2. What is Tim going to do next?

3. What is Emily going to do next?

Answers

1. They are putting all the stuff away first.

2. He's going to clean the bathrooms.

3. She's going to put in a load of laundry.

#38: How to Split Chores

Bobby and Min are talking about splitting chores.

Bobby: Min, can I talk to you about chores? I'm doing more than my fair share. I do all the cooking and laundry and end up doing most of the cleaning too.

Min: I know. You're right. I'm sorry. I've been so busy at work that when I get home, I just want to relax.

Bobby: Is there a way to make this fairer?

Min: Why don't we make a chart? I think I'd do better if I knew the things I was 100% responsible for. Right now, it's just not on my mind. Like every Saturday, I clean the bathrooms. Or, I have to cook dinner on Tuesday and Thursday night.

Bobby: Sure, we can do that.

Min: Thanks for bringing this up. I don't want you to feel like you have to do everything.

Check Your Understanding

1. Who currently does most of the chores?

2. What does Min propose?

3. Why doesn't Min do enough chores?

Answers

1. Bobby does most of the chores.

2. She suggests that they make a chore chart.

3. She doesn't do that many chores because she's busy at work and just wants to relax at home.

#39: Talking about Holidays

Sarah and Lucy are talking about holidays.

Sarah: Didn't you just get back from Bali? How was it?

Lucy: So amazing. Everyone needs to go there! It was the best vacation I've ever taken.

Sarah: What did you like so much?

Lucy: First of all, it was so beautiful. And the food. Plus the spas and massages. There wasn't anything I didn't like about it.

Sarah: Awesome! I'm happy that you had such a great time. I need a vacation too!

Lucy: You've been working too hard lately.

Check Your Understanding

1. What did Lucy think about Bali?
2. What things does Lucy mention liking?
3. Has Sarah been on vacation lately?

Answers

1. She loved it.
2. She liked the food, the natural beauty, and the spas and massages.
3. No, she hasn't.

#40: Vacation Plans

Kevin and Tony are talking about their plans.

Kevin: What are you doing for summer vacation?

Tony: Well, I just booked some camping time.

Kevin: Where are you headed?

Tony: To Cultus Lake. It's beautiful there plus there are waterslides for the kids and a pub for me!

Kevin: That sounds just about perfect. I'm going to do a mini stay-cation and do lots of day hikes and stuff like that.

Tony: Sounds nice too. Where do you like hiking?

Kevin: I'm just getting into it now. I bought a book though so I'll do some stuff from there.

Check Your Understanding

1. What is Tony doing for summer vacation?
2. Is Kevin an experienced hiker?
3. What can the kids do at Cultus Lake?

Answers

1. He's going camping with his family.
2. No, he's a beginner.
3. They can go on the waterslides.

#41: Talking about a New Neighbor

Kevin and Emily are talking about a new neighbor.

Kevin: Did you hear that our new neighbor is moving in on Saturday?

Emily: Oh, exciting. Do you know anything about him?

Kevin: I think it's a woman with her 6-year old daughter.

Emily: Good! I was hoping we wouldn't have a partier!

Kevin: Oh no. I don't think so. I'll go introduce myself on Saturday.

Emily: Me too. See you around.

Check Your Understanding

1. When is the new neighbor moving in?
2. How many people are moving in?
3. Why is Emily happy that there's a child?

Answers

1. She is moving in on Saturday.
2. Two people are moving in.
3. She's happy because she thinks that they won't be loud.

#42: Another New Neighbor

Bob and Sam are talking about their new neighbor.

Bob: Have you met Sidney yet?

Sam: I've seen her here and there but we haven't said more than hi. What's she like?

Bob: Carrie seems nice. A way better neighbor than Tony!

Sam: Okay, good. I'm happy to never have to talk to that guy again. He was so obnoxious and rude.

Bob: Same here. I hated running into Tony. Carrie is friendly and easy to talk to.

Sam: That's a relief.

Check Your Understanding

1. Who has met the new neighbor?
2. Why didn't they like Tony?
3. Are they happy to have a new neighbor?

Answers

1. Bob has met the new neighbor.
2. They didn't like Tony because he was obnoxious and rude.
3. Yes, they are.

#43: At the Movie Theater

Peter and Liz are at the movie theater and talking about which movie to see.

Peter: What shows look good to you?

Liz: Let's see. What starts around 7:00? Maybe Spiderman or that new drama that everyone is talking about.

Peter: I don't like dramas that much but Spiderman sounds great.

Liz: Okay, it starts in about 20 minutes. That's perfect. Let's get some tickets.

Peter: Sounds good. It's my treat! Didn't you buy me dinner last time we hung out?

Liz: I did. Thanks for remembering.

Check Your Understanding

1. Why is Peter paying for the movie?
2. Which movie are they seeing?
3. What kind of movies does Peter dislike?

Answers

1. He's paying for the movie because Liz recently bought him dinner.
2. They are watching Spiderman.
3. He doesn't like dramas.

#44: Getting Snacks at the Movie Theater

Mason and Allan are talking about getting snacks at the movie theater.

Mason: Let's get some snacks and drinks before we go in.

Allan: Sure, let's see...a small popcorn is $6.25 and an extra-large is $9.50. Why don't we share a big one? It's a way better value.

Mason: Good plan. But, do you like the BBQ salt shaker thing? It's my favourite.

Allan: I've never tried it but I love BBQ chips so I'm sure I'll like it.

Mason: You get the popcorn and I'll get us each a drink. What would you like?

Allan: A medium coke, please.

Check Your Understanding

1. Why are they sharing a popcorn?
2. Who is buying the popcorn?
3. What drink does Allan want?

Answers

1. They are sharing a larger popcorn because it's a better value.
2. Allan is buying the popcorn.
3. He wants a medium coke.

#45: At the Cafe

Heidi is ordering a drink.

Heidi: Hi, can I please get a caramel macchiato with an extra shot of espresso?

Barista: Sure, what size would you like?

Heidi: A medium.

Barista: Can I have your name, please?

Heidi: I'm Heidi.

Barista: Okay, that'll be $4.55.

Heidi: Sure.

Check Your Understanding

1. What size of drink does Heidi want?
2. Does Heidi want her drink strong or weak?
3. Is her drink less than $5?

Answers

1. She wants a medium.
2. She wants her drink strong.
3. Yes, her drink is less than $5.

#46: Deciding What to Order

Cindy and Mary are talking about what they're going to order.

Cindy: I never go to fancy coffee shops! What do you usually get here?

Mary: I go simple and usually get a cappuccino. They do a great job of it.

Cindy: Okay, I'll get that with almond milk. I'm kind of hungry. I think I'll get something to eat too.

Mary: They have some nice grilled sandwiches. I usually get the pesto, tomato and mozzarella one.

Cindy: Amazing. I'll take your recommendation on that one too. Thanks for your help!

Mary: No problem.

Check Your Understanding

1. Who doesn't usually go to fancy coffee shops?

2. What is Cindy getting to eat and drink?

3. Has Mary been to this coffee shop before?

Answers

1. Cindy rarely goes to fancy coffee shops.

2. She's getting a cappuccino with almond milk and a grilled sandwich.

3. Yes, she has been there before.

#47: Making a Special Order at a Restaurant

Nicole is checking to see if something is vegan.

Nicole: I'd like to get the Pad Thai with tofu but I'm a vegan. Does it have fish sauce?

Waiter: Pad Thai usually does I think. Let me check with the cook.

Nicole: Sure, thank you.

Waiter: He said that it normally does but he can make yours without it.

Nicole: Okay. I'll have that then plus the spring rolls but with no shrimp.

Waiter: Sure. They're already vegan actually. Anything else?

Nicole: No, that's everything. Thank you.

Check Your Understanding

1. Where is Nicole?
2. What does she not want to eat?
3. What did she order?

Answers

1. She is at a Thai restaurant.
2. She's a vegan so she doesn't want any fish sauce or shrimp in her meal.
3. She ordered Pad Thai with tofu and spring rolls.

#48: Gluten-Free Options

Tommy is enquiring about gluten-free options.

Tommy: I'm gluten-free so wondering what I can eat here. It's a serious allergy.

Waiter: There are a few things that'll work for you. We can make all of our pizzas gluten-free quite easily. And for all the burgers and sandwiches, we have a gluten-free option for an extra $1.

Tommy: The meat on your pizzas doesn't have gluten in it?

Waiter: Oh, I'm not sure about that. Which pizza were you interested in?

Tommy: The pepperoni.

Waiter: Let me go check the package....okay...no gluten!

Tommy: Sure, I'll get that then.

Check Your Understanding

1. What can't Tommy eat?
2. Does the pepperoni have gluten in it?
3. What are the things he can eat at that restaurant?

Answers

1. He can't eat things with gluten.
2. No, it doesn't.
3. He can get a pizza, burger or sandwich.

#49: A Suspicious Person

Kerry and Virginia are talking about a suspicious guy in the neighborhood.

Kerry: What's that guy doing? I've seen him walk by here at least five times in the past hour.

Virginia: I've seen him around a lot too. Maybe he's planning on breaking into Ed and Cindy's house while they're on vacation.

Kerry: Maybe. What should we do?

Virginia: I think we should call the police. They can come talk to him and scare him off hopefully.

Kerry: Okay, I'll call now.

Virginia: And I'll keep an eye on him to see where he goes.

Check Your Understanding

1. How many times has Kerry seen the suspicious man?

2. What do they think he's going to do?

3. What are they going to do?

Answers

1. He's seen him at least five times in an hour.

2. They think he might break into their neighbor's house.

3. They're going to call the police.

#50: The New Guy

Eddy and Ethan are talking about a new guy at work.

Eddy: Have you met Bob yet?

Ethan: Oh yeah. He's already kind of infamous.

Eddy: I know. He's a weird guy. I got a super bad vibe from him. We had the strangest conversation about guns at lunch the other day.

Ethan: Same here. I don't have a good feeling about him. He seems pretty sketchy.

Eddy: I'm keeping my eye on him for sure.

Ethan: I heard that he's a genius at computer programming though. I guess that's why they hired him.

Eddy: That must be it. It's certainly not because of his personality!

Check Your Understanding

1. Do they like Bob?

2. Why did Bob likely get hired?

3. What did Eddy and Bob talk about at lunch?

Answers

1. No, they don't like Bob.

2. He probably got hired because of his computer programming skills.

3. They talked about guns.

#51: Talking About an Accident

Sam and Kerry are talking about an accident.

Sam: Oh Kerry! What happened?

Kerry: I hit a rock while riding my bike and went over the handlebars.

Sam: Oh no! It looks bad.

Kerry: I had to go to the ER. I hit my head pretty hard but no serious damage because I was wearing a helmet. Just a cut on my leg and some scrapes on my hands.

Sam: Thank god for that. How did you not break any bones?

Kerry: I'm not sure. It's a small miracle I think. They did an x-ray of my entire body to check and I also got a CAT scan of my head which was interesting. They were worried about bleeding in my brain.

Sam: I'm happy to hear that you're okay!

Check Your Understanding

1. How did Kerry get hurt?

2. Were Kerry's injuries serious?

3. Did the doctors think Kerry might have serious injuries?

Answers

1. He fell off his bike.

2. No, they weren't.

3. Yes, they did. They thought he might have bleeding in his brain.

#52: A Recent Accident

Joanna and Janice are talking about a recent accident.

Joanna: Hey, how are you doing? I heard that you got into a car accident recently.

Janice: Yes. I got rear-ended a couple of weeks ago.

Joanna: Was it serious?

Janice: There wasn't that much damage to my car but I did get whiplash. I'm still recovering and have to go to physio all the time. The car behind me wasn't moving that fast, only about 20 km/hour.

Joanna: That's tough for sure. Did you get some money from insurance for it?

Janice: Not yet. It's still too early for that. I have to recover from my injuries first.

Check Your Understanding

1. What bad thing happened to Janice?

2. When did the accident happen?

3. What injury did she get?

Answers

1. She got into a car accident.

2. It happened about two weeks ago.

3. She got whiplash.

#53: Talking about Hobbies

Keith and Jenny are on a first date and are talking about their hobbies.

Keith: So what do you like to do for fun?

Jenny: Mostly anything outside. In the summer, I like hiking or kayaking. And then in the winter, I ski or snowshoe.

Keith: So many things! I love kayaking. What are some of your favourite places to go?

Jenny: I usually stay local and go to the Alouette River or Rocky Point. What about you?

Keith: I live pretty close to UBC so I go to Spanish Banks or Jericho Beach. But it can sometimes get pretty windy there.

Jenny: I've heard that. That's why I like the Alouette River. It's not as bad on windy days.

Check Your Understanding

1. What is their similar hobby?

2. What is the negative thing about kayaking at Spanish Banks?

3. Where does Jenny go kayaking?

Answers

1. They both like kayaking.

2. It can sometimes get windy there.

3. She usually goes to places near her house.

#54: Talking about Hiking

Tommy and Sam are talking about hiking.

Tommy: What did you get up to this weekend?

Sam: Oh, I went on a big hiking trip to Golden Ears.

Tommy: That's such a nice place, right?

Sam: It was my first time there actually. It was certainly amazing and I'd love to go camping there as well. Do you go there a lot?

Tommy: It's not that far from my house so I go at least once a month. I've done almost all the trails there.

Sam: Nice. Let's go hiking together sometime. I'd love to try Evans Peak.

Tommy: I'd love to. Maybe next weekend if you're free?

Check Your Understanding

1. Who has been to Golden Ears many times?

2. Where does Sam want to hike to?

3. Who lives close to Golden Ears?

Answers

1. Tommy has been to Golden Ears many times.

2. He'd like to hike Evans Peak.

3. Tommy lives near Golden Ears.

#55:Talking about Pets

Tina and Craig run into each other while out walking their dogs.
Tina: Hi Craig. I didn't know that you had a dog.
Craig: Oh, I don't. My son is on vacation and I'm looking after this guy for a couple of weeks. His name is Bingo.
Tina: Oh, lucky you. He's a cutie.
Craig: Yeah, he's such a nice dog. He's super friendly with kids and never growls or barks.
Tina: I wish. My guy here doesn't like other dogs or people! I tried to train him but no luck.
Craig: Have you tried dog training school? It worked for a friend of mine.
Tina: No, I'll have to check into that.

Check Your Understanding

1. Is Bingo a nice dog?

2. Is Bingo Craig's dog?

3. Is Tina's dog friendly?

Answers

1. Yes, he's a very nice dog.

2. No, Bingo is his son's dog.

3. No, it isn't.

#56: A New Dog

Bob and Ed are talking about Ed getting a new dog.

Bob: How are you doing? I heard that your sweet dog died a couple of months ago.

Ed: It's still sad but he was 15 years old and lived a good life. Sammy and I are thinking about getting a puppy. We miss having a pet.

Bob: Oh, that's exciting. Any idea what kind?

Ed: No plan yet. We'll probably go to the shelter and get a mutt.

Bob: Lots of dogs there need homes for sure.

Ed: Exactly. I don't like buying pets from pet stores or breeders.

Check Your Understanding

1. Why is Ed thinking about getting a puppy?
2. Where will Ed get a new dog?
3. How old was Ed's dog when it died?

Answers

1. His old dog died and he misses having a pet.
2. He'll get a dog from the shelter.
3. It was 15.

#57: Talking About the Weather

Tina and Ed are talking about an upcoming storm.

Tina: Did you see the forecast? They're predicting a huge snowstorm for Friday afternoon.

Ed: I heard that. I was thinking of taking the day off work. I don't want to get caught out in it.

Tina: Same here. The roads will be treacherous.

Ed: They definitely will be, especially with the budget cutbacks! The city barely has any snowplows. It takes them hours to clear even the main roads.

Tina: I know, right? I've noticed that recently too.

Ed: Well, stay safe and let me know if you need anything. I have a 4x4 truck so can come rescue you if you need.

Tina: Sure thing. Thank you. I'm stocked up on food and water though so I can just stay home.

Check Your Understanding

1. What is happening on Friday afternoon?

2. Is Ed going to work on Friday?

3. How did Tina get ready for the storm?

Answers

1. There will be a big snowstorm.

2. He might take the day off on Friday.

3. She bought extra food and water.

#58: A Heatwave

Zed and Tim are talking about the recent heatwave.

Zed: Did you hear that we might break the heat record for today?

Tim: Oh wow. What's the temperature supposed to be?

Zed: They're predicting 37 degrees!

Tim: That's insane. You know where I'll be. At the movie theater the entire day. That's too hot to even go to the beach.

Zed: For real. Thankfully I have air conditioning at my house. Come over for a beer if you want.

Tim: I may take you up on that offer! Are you serious?

Zed: Sure, come over this afternoon after lunch if you want.

Check Your Understanding

1. What will the weather be like today?

2. Who has air conditioning at their house?

3. What is Tim's plan for the day?

Answers

1. It will be extremely hot.

2. Zed has air conditioning at his house.

3. He planned to go to the movie theater but he may go over to Zed's house.

#59: Talking About a New Phone

Min-Guy is asking Shuo for some advice about getting a new phone.

Min-Gyu: Hey Shuo, you're up to date on the latest technology. Maybe you can help me. I'm thinking about getting a new phone.

Shuo: Ah, what do you have now?

Min-Gyu: An iPhone but it's old and slow now. I want something new.

Shuo: Are you happy with the iPhone or are you considering switching?

Min-Gyu: What do you think?

Shuo: Well, the Samsung phones are nice and have more bang for the buck. You pay a premium for Apple stuff.

Min-Guy: I'm open to switching. Do you have a model recommendation?

Shuo: Let me look into it a bit and I'll text you later, okay?

Check Your Understanding

1. Why is Min-Gyu asking Shuo for advice?

2. What brand of phone is the better value?

3. Did Shuo have a specific phone to recommend?

Answers

1. He's asking for her advice because she's up-to-date on technology.

2. Samsung phones offer better value.

3. Not yet. She has to do more research about it.

#60: Bob's New Phone

Bob and Jenny are talking about Bob's new phone.

Jenny: Bob. What's that flashy new thing you're holding there?

Bob: Oh, it's the latest iPhone.

Jenny: How did you get it? I thought there was a waiting list.

Bob: Exactly. I got on the waiting list the day it became available.

Jenny: Lucky you! Is it worth the hype?

Bob: It's pretty impressive but I can't imagine waiting in line for it! It is certainly better than my old iPhone.

Jenny: Nice. I'm thinking about getting one but it's a bit out of my price range.

Bob: I know. It's too much money for what it is. But, I don't care! I still bought it.

Check Your Understanding

1. Is the new iPhone expensive?

2. Is the new phone popular?

3. Is Jenny going to get the new iPhone?

Answers

1. Yes, it's very expensive.

2. Yes, it's difficult to get.

3. She's considering it but it's a bit expensive for her.

#61: Talking About an Upcoming Wedding

Sam and Ken are talking about a wedding.

Sam: Did you hear that Tina and Craig are getting married?

Ken: When did that happen?

Sam: They got engaged last month.

Ken: How did I not know about it? When is the wedding?

Sam: This summer. I think in August.

Ken: Oh nice! I don't think I'll get invited but you for sure will. I would love to go though. It'd be fun to see the old gang from high school.

Sam: I'm sure I will. Craig and I have been friends since high school.

Ken: Want to take me as your date?

Check Your Understanding

1. Who is getting married?

2. Who will probably get invited to the wedding?

3. When is the wedding?

Answers

1. Tina and Craig are getting married.

2. Sam will probably get invited.

3. The wedding is in August.

#62: Going to a Wedding

Ward and Tracy are talking about whether or not to go to a friend's wedding.

Tracy: Did you see the mail? We got a wedding invitation for Tom and Tina's wedding.

Ward: Oh, when is it?

Tracy: August 2nd. It's a Saturday.

Ward: Do we have any plans yet for that weekend?

Tracy: Not yet. I think we should go! I'd love to take a trip to Kelowna.

Ward: Sounds perfect. Let's get our hotel booked before it gets too busy. Why don't we spend a couple of extra days there? Maybe Friday to Monday?

Tracy: Sure, why don't you take care of that and I'll let Tom know that we can come.

Check Your Understanding

1. Are Tracy and Ward going to the wedding?

2. Where is the wedding happening?

3. Who will book the hotel?

Answers

1. Yes, they are planning on going.

2. The wedding is in Kelowna.

3. Ward will book the hotel.

#63: Talking About Health Problems

Emily is talking to Mabel, her grandmother on the phone about her health problems.

Emily: Hi Grandma, how are feeling today?

Mabel: Honestly, not great. My legs hurt so much today. I went for a walk yesterday but overdid it I think.

Emily: Oh no. How far did you go?

Mabel: Well, to the mall and back.

Emily: Grandma! That's too far. Call me if you need to go there. I can take you.

Mabel: Okay, I will next time but I don't like to bother anyone.

Emily: It's no problem at all. I'd love to help you. You shouldn't walk that far anymore.

Check Your Understanding

1. How is Mabel feeling today?

2. Did Mabel go for a long walk yesterday?

3. Why was Mabel reluctant to ask for a ride to the mall?

Answers

1. She has sore legs.

2. Yes, she did.

3. She was reluctant because she didn't want to bother anyone.

#64: Talking about Health Problems

Madison and Sara are talking about health problems.

Madison: Hey Sara, how are you doing? I heard that you were in the hospital.

Sara: I was for a few days. I had a weird stomach thing going on. It turned out to be nothing but it was super painful.

Madison: What did the doctors say? They couldn't find anything?

Sara: They did all these tests but nothing came up. And then it just got better after a few days. It was strange.

Madison: That does sound odd. Well, I'm happy you're feeling better now.

Sara: Me too. It's impossible to sleep in the hospital. I was getting so tired.

Madison: I hope it doesn't happen again.

Check Your Understanding

1. Who was in the hospital?
2. What was wrong with Sara?
3. Why didn't Sara like staying in the hospital?

Answers

1. Sara was in the hospital.
2. She has a painful stomach but the doctors don't know why.
3. She didn't like it because it was difficult to sleep there.

#65: Talking About a Teacher

Timmy and Matt (high school students) are talking about who their new teacher will be.

Timmy: Did you find out who your homeroom teacher will be for next year?

Matt: No. I don't know. How did you find out?

Timmy: You can call the school. The secretary will tell you.

Matt: Okay. I'll do that later. Who is your teacher?

Timmy: Mr. Smith.

Matt: Tough break. I've heard that he's super strict. I hope I don't get him but I'd love to be in your class.

Timmy: I know. I'm not that excited about it. Well, find out and let me know.

Matt: I will when I get home!

Check Your Understanding

1. How can you find out who your new teacher will be?

2. Is Timmy happy with his new teacher?

3. Are Timmy and Matt in the same class?

Answers

1. You can phone the school and the secretary will tell you.

2. No, he isn't.

3. They don't know yet. Matt doesn't know who his teacher is.

#66: The English Teacher

Sam and Andy are talking about their English teacher.

Sam: How did you do on your essay?

Andy: Not great. I got a C.

Sam: What happened?

Andy: Well, Mrs. Brown said I had too many simple grammar mistakes. Honestly. I didn't think it was so bad. How did you do?

Sam: Not much better. I got a C+. She said the same thing about my paper.

Andy: She's so strict with her grading. I wonder if anyone got an A? We're two of the best students in the class.

Sam: My guess is that nobody ever gets an A in her class.

Check Your Understanding

1. Did they do well on their essay?
2. Why did they get poor scores on their essays?
3. What do they think about Mrs. Brown's grading?

Answers

1. No, they didn't.
2. They got poor scores because they had too many grammar mistakes.
3. They think she grades strictly.

#67: Talking about Getting to School

Min and Bobby are talking about how they get to school.

Min: How are you doing Bobby?

Bobby: Okay but I'm super tired.

Min: Why? A bad sleep?

Bobby: No, just a short one. I have to commute for two hours each way so early morning classes are the worst for me.

Min: Where do you live?

Bobby: Oh, I live in Maple Ridge.

Min: Tough break. That's terrible.

Bobby: I know, but I live with my parents for free so I can save money. It's not all bad.

Check Your Understanding

1. Why does Bobby live so far away from school?

2. How long does it take Bobby to get to school?

3. How is Bobby feeling today?

Answers

1. He lives so far away because it's free.

2. It takes him two hours.

3. He's very tired.

#68: Traffic

Gary and Edgar are talking about the traffic.

Gary: I'm surprised that I made it to class on time!

Edgar: What happened?

Gary: Well, I left a few minutes late which isn't a big deal but then there was way more traffic than normal.

Edgar: I noticed that too. I usually grab a coffee before class but I had no time. I just had to rush here.

Gary: I wonder what happened? Did you hear?

Edgar: I tried to find out on the radio but didn't hear anything.

Gary: Probably an accident of some kind but I didn't see anything.

Check Your Understanding

1. What does Edgar usually do before class?
2. Did Gary make it to class on time?
3. Why was there more traffic than usual?

Answers

1. He usually gets a coffee.
2. Yes, he did.
3. They're not sure why there was more traffic.

#69: Help With Moving

Jenny is helping Tom move.

Tom: Thanks for your help with moving today, Jenny. You shouldn't have gone to the trouble.

Jenny: Oh, no problem at all. I don't mind helping you. You've been very kind to me over the years.

Tom: You're welcome. And, I still appreciate the help.

Jenny: No worries. That's what friends are for.

Tom: What are you doing tomorrow? Why don't I buy you dinner?

Jenny: Nothing. That sounds great.

Check your Understanding

1. What is Tom doing?
2. How will Tom repay Jenny for her help?
3. How long have they known each other?

Answers

1. He is moving.
2. He will buy her dinner the next day.
3. They've known each other for years.

#70: Help with an Assignment

Carrie is helping Tim with an assignment.

Tim: Carrie, I appreciate your help with that assignment.

Carrie: No problem, it was a tough one. It took me a long time to do it.

Tim: Yeah, I just couldn't figure it out. I spent 10 hours on it but made no progress.

Carrie: Anyway, I'm always happy to help a friend out. You've done the same for me many times!

Tim: I'm thankful to have you in this class with me.

Carrie: I feel the same way.

Check your Understanding

1. Is the assignment difficult?
2. How do Tim and Carrie know each other?
3. Is this the first time they've worked together on an assignment?

Answers

1. Yes, it's very difficult.
2. They are in the same class at school.
3. No, they've done it many times in the past.

#71: Bumping into Someone

Carrie and Tim bumped into each other at the grocery store.

Tim: Carrie! Long time, no see.

Carrie: Wow, it has been a while, right? Maybe a year?

Tim: Yeah, I think it was around Christmas last year that I ran into you at the mall.

Carrie: That's right. I remember that. How are you?

Tim: Oh good. Just busy at work. Nothing new. How about you?

Carrie: I got a new dog and we've been having so much fun with him.

Tim: Nice! Anyway, nice to see you again! I gotta run pick up Tony from soccer pretty soon.

Carrie: For sure. Let's catch up over coffee soon.

Check your Understanding

1. When was the last time they saw each other?

2. Why can't Tim stay and talk?

3. Is Tim busy at work?

Answers

1. It was about a year ago.

2. He has to pick up his son at soccer soon.

3. Yes, he is.

#72: Turn Up the Music

Tom can't hear well and wants to turn up the music.

Tom: Do you mind if I turn up the music? I love this song. I can't hear that well in my old age!

Jenny: No, go ahead. It's fine with me. It is a bit quiet for me as well.

Tom: I'd love to turn the heat up a bit too. It's freezing in here.

Jenny: Sure, I can do that. It'll take a while to heat up though. Do you want to borrow a sweater or a blanket?

Tom: I'd love that blanket, please. I don't know what's wrong with me. I'm always cold these days.

Jenny: Are you feeling okay? Maybe something is going on?

Tom: I don't know. I just had a check-up at the doctor and everything was good.

Check your Understanding

1. What are Tom's problems?

2. Is Tom sick?

3. Does Tom borrow a sweater from Jenny?

Answers

1. He can't hear the music well and he's also cold.

2. No, he isn't.

3. No, he doesn't. He borrows a blanket.

#73: The Sleepover

Tim is asking his Mom if he can have a sleepover at his friend's house.

Tim: Hey Mom, can I stay at Tony's house tonight? He just invited me.

Carrie: Are his parents going to be home?

Tim: Of course they are!

Carrie: It is a school night though, right? I don't think that's a good idea.

Tim: No, remember it's a holiday tomorrow. It's a day off because of parent-teacher interviews.

Carrie: Oh, that's right. I forgot about that. Sure, you can. I'll give his parents a quick call first though. What time will you go over?

Tim: He said to come over for dinner so maybe around 6:00.

Carrie: Okay. I can give you a ride.

Check your Understanding

1. Does Tim have school tomorrow?

2. Is Tim allowed to go to the sleepover?

3. When is Tim going over to his friend's house?

Answers

1. No, he doesn't.

2. Yes, he is but his Mom will call Tony's parents first.

3. He will go over at 6:00.

#74: A Ride to the Airport

Tom is going to give Jenny a ride to the airport.

Tom: Hey Jenny, do you need a ride to the airport? Aren't you going to Tokyo tomorrow?

Jenny: Yes, I am. Oh, if you wouldn't mind. I'd appreciate it. I was going to take the subway but this is way better!

Tom: Sure, I don't mind lending you a hand. What time is your flight?

Jenny: Thank you. My flight leaves at noon. So, I'd like to get there around 9:30 which means that we should leave here around 9:00. Does that sound okay?

Tom: Sure, that's fine. I'll pick you up at 9:00 then.

Jenny: Okay, see you tomorrow.

Check your Understanding

1. Where is Jenny going tomorrow?

2. When is Tom going to pick her up?

3. How long does it take to get to the airport?

Answers

1. She is going to Tokyo.

2. He'll pick her up at 9:00.

3. It takes about 30 minutes.

#75: Catching a Movie

Tim and Carrie are talking about what they're going to do this weekend.

Tim: Hey Carrie, do you want to catch a movie this weekend?

Carrie: Honestly, I'm a little short on cash these days. How about staying in and watching a movie at my house?

Tim: Sure, that sounds great too. There's this new one that just came out on Netflix that everyone is talking about.

Carrie: Awesome! I'll make some snacks for us.

Tim: Sure. I'll bring some wine. What time should I come over?

Carrie: Why don't you come over at 7:30?

Tim: Perfect. I'll see you then.

Check your Understanding

1. Where are they going to watch a movie?

2. What is Tim going to bring?

3. Why doesn't Carrie want to go to the movie theater?

Answers

1. They are going to watch it at Carrie's house.

2. He's going to bring a bottle of wine.

3. She doesn't want to go to the movie theater because it's expensive and she doesn't have a lot of money right now.

#76: Some Sad News

Tom just heard that his grandmother died.

Tom: I got some sad news last night. I heard that my grandmother died.

Jenny: Oh no, I'm so sorry to hear that. What happened?

Tom: She had been sick for a while but she had a stroke last night

Jenny: Ahhh, that's too bad my friend. Were you close?

Tom: We weren't that close but I'll miss her. I used to see her every couple of years.

Jenny: Anything I can do to help? Want to grab a coffee and talk?

Tom: Not right now. I feel like being alone. But, I'll let you know, okay?

Check your Understanding

1. What is Tom's bad news?

2. Was her death a surprise?

3. Does Tom want to be around people now?

Answers

1. His bad news is that his grandmother died.

2. No, she had been sick for a while.

3. No, he wants to spend some time alone.

#77: A Terrible Cold

Carrie can't go hiking because she's sick.

Tim: Do you want to go for a quick hike after work today?

Carrie: Oh, I can't. I have a terrible cold.

Tim: Oh no! Did you stay home from work today?

Carrie: Yes. For the past three days.

Tim: Oh friend. That's terrible. Are you getting any better?

Carrie: Yes, today was the first time I got out of bed.

Tim: Do you need me to bring you anything?

Carrie: My Mom brought over some homemade soup a couple of days ago. I'm doing okay. And I just got some groceries delivered.

Check your Understanding

1. How long has Carrie been sick?

2. Does Carrie need Tim's help?

3. What did Carrie's Mom bring her?

Answers

1. She's been sick for at least three days.

2. No, she doesn't.

3. She brought her some homemade soup.

#78: Signing up for a Class

Tim wants to sign up for a fitness class.

Tim: Do you have any fitness classes scheduled?

Clerk: Yes, the classes are listed online or you can have a look here.

Tim: I'm most interested in spin classes. Do you have any of those?

Clerk: Yes, we do. There is at least one of those classes almost every day.

Tim: Great. How can I sign up?

Clerk: Online, or with me now.

Tim: Okay. Do you have any starting in the next half hour?

Clerk: Yes, there's one in 15 minutes. Do you want to sign up?

Tim: Sure, and then one for Tuesday as well.

Check your Understanding

1. What kind of class is Tim interested in?

2. Is Tim going to do a spin class today?

3. How can you sign up for a class?

Answers

1. He's interested in a spin class.

2. Yes, he is.

3. You can sign up with the person at the desk or online.

#79: At the Library

Tom is at the library and needs some help.

Tom: Hi, it's my first time here. I have a few questions.

Clerk: Sure, how can I help?

Tom: How many books can I take out at a time?

Clerk: You can take out up to 20 books.

Tom: And how long can I keep them?

Clerk: 3 weeks for books and 2 weeks for movies and music.

Tom: Finally, do you have a quiet study space?

Clerk: Unfortunately no, but it's usually pretty quiet between 10:00 and 2:00.

Tom: Okay. Can I bring coffee in with me?

Clerk: Sure, that's fine. As long as it's in a closed container.

Check your Understanding

1. How many books can you check out?

2. What's the quietest time at the library?

3. Are you allowed to bring drinks into the library?

Answers

1. You can check out 20 books.

2. It's quiet between 10:00 and 2:00.

3. Yes, you are.

#80: At the Coffee Shop

Carrie is ordering a drink.

Barista: Hi, what can I get you?

Carrie: What do you recommend? I don't like coffee that much.

Barista: Sure. We have lots of options. Do you want a hot or cold drink?

Carrie: Hot, please.

Barista: Sure, we have some nice teas or hot chocolate.

Carrie: Okay, I'll have a hot chocolate then.

Barista: What size would you like?

Carrie: I'll have a large.

Barista: Is it for here or to go?

Carrie: For here, please.

Check your Understanding

1. Does Carrie drink coffee?

2. What size hot chocolate does Carrie get?

3. Does the coffee shop have things besides coffee?

Answers

1. No, she doesn't.

2. She gets a large hot chocolate.

3. Yes, it does.

#81: At the Dentist

Carrie is talking about her teeth with the dentist.

Dentist: How's your brushing and flossing going? Your x-ray shows two new cavities.

Carrie: I brush almost every time after I eat.

Dentist: And your flossing?

Carrie: Well, not so great. Maybe once a week.

Dentist: Okay. That's not ideal. You should be doing it every night before bed. It's easy for food to get stuck between teeth and cause cavities.

Carrie: I know. I'll do better.

Dentist: Just make it a habit. Do it every day for 30 days and you'll never forget!

Check your Understanding

1. Is Carrie good at flossing her teeth?
2. What causes cavities?
3. What does the dentist recommend?

Answers

1. No, she only does it once a week.
2. Food getting stuck between teeth can cause cavities.
3. She recommends flossing every day before bed.

#82: Getting a Beer After Work

Tim and Carrie are talking about their plan for after work.

Tim: Let's grab a beer after work. I need to chill out.

Carrie: I know, it's been a long day. I'm up for it.

Tim: Awesome! Should we invite Bob and Jen?

Carrie: Sure, why not?

Tim: Okay, I'll ask them.

Carrie: Cool, let's walk over to the Dublin together around 5:00.

Tim: That's perfect. I'll stop by your desk on my way out.

Check your Understanding

1. How many people are going to get a beer after work?
2. Where are they going for a beer?
3. Who's desk is closest to the exit?

Answers

1. At least two people are getting a beer but maybe three or four.
2. They are going to a pub named the Dublin.
3. Carrie's desk is closer to the exit.

#83: Burgers for Dinner

Tim and Carrie are talking about what kind of burgers to make.

Tim: I'm thinking of making burgers for dinner tonight. How does that sound to you?

Carrie: Great. I love burgers.

Tim: Okay. I have a few different kinds in the freezer: beef, turkey, or veggie. What would you like?

Carrie: Oh, what kind of veggie ones are they?

Tim: Some black bean ones that I got at Costco.

Carrie: Oh, those are delicious. I'll have one of those, please.

Tim: Good choice! What should I have? Hmmm. I think I'll also go with a veggie one.

Check your Understanding

1. What kind of burgers are they having?

2. Does Carrie like all kinds of veggie burgers?

3. How many kinds of burgers does Tim have in the freezer?

Answers

1. They are both having veggie burgers.

2. She probably doesn't like all kinds of veggie burgers.

3. He has three kinds.

#84: Another Date

Tom and Jenny are talking about another date.

Tom: I had a good time getting to know you. Are you interested in going out with me again?

Jenny: Yes, I'd love to. How about this weekend?

Tom: Sure, that sounds good.

Jenny: Perfect. What should we do?

Tom: The weather looks great for Saturday. What about going for a hike?

Jenny: Sure. I love hiking. How about Grouse Mountain?

Tom: Perfect. I'll pick you up around 1:00?

Jenny: Sure. See you then.

Check your Understanding

1. How many dates have Tom and Jenny been on?

2. Do they like each other?

3. How's the weather looking for Saturday?

Answers

1. They've probably been on only one date.

2. Yes, they do. They are going on another date.

3. It's going to be nice outside on Saturday.

#85: Bad Weather for the Weekend

Tom and Jenny are talking about their weekend plans.

Tom: Hey Jenny, what are you up to this weekend?

Jenny: Oh, not much. I think the weather is going to be terrible. Maybe some cooking and Netflix. How about you?

Tom: That sounds nice. I go hiking in all weather, so I'll probably do that on Saturday.

Jenny: Wow. You're braver than me! Where are you going to go?

Tom: Probably along the Seymour River. There are lots of trees so it's not so bad, even in the rain. You should come with me.

Jenny: Okay. I should get a bit of exercise.

Check your Understanding

1. Does Jenny like going outside in terrible weather?

2. Does Tom go hiking even in the rain?

3. Is Jenny going to go hiking with Tom this weekend?

Answers

1. No, she doesn't.

2. Yes, he does.

3. Yes, she is.

#86: New Shoes

Tom is looking for some Air Jordans.

Tom: Excuse me, I'm looking for the Air Jordans in a size 8.5.

Clerk: Hmmm...let me check for you. Just a second. I'm not sure we have that size left. They're super popular.

Tom: Sure.

Clerk: Okay, I see that we should have a couple of pairs. Let me grab one for you to try on. What color were you interested in? We have black or white.

Tom: I'd love the black ones, please.

Clerk: Okay, I'll go get those. I'll be back in a minute.

Tom: Sure, thanks.

Check your Understanding

1. What color of shoes does Tom want?

2. Does the store have a lot of Air Jordans?

3. Does the store have the size that Tom needs?

Answers

1. He wants to get the black shoes.

2. No, they don't.

3. Yes, they do.

#87: Getting a Refund

Tom would like to get his money back.

Tom: I'd like to exchange this t-shirt, please.

Clerk: Is there anything wrong with it?

Tom: Oh no, I bought it for my daughter but she doesn't like the color.

Clerk: Okay, I see. Do you have the receipt?

Tom: Yes, right here.

Clerk: Okay, would you like a refund or would you like to exchange it?

Tom: A refund is great.

Clerk: Do you have the credit card you bought it with?

Tom: Yes, I do.

Check your Understanding

1. Why is Tom returning the shirt?

2. How did Tom pay for the t-shirt?

3. Does Tom want his money back?

Answers

1. He is returning the shirt because his daughter didn't like the color.

2. He paid with a credit card.

3. Yes, he does.

#88: Ordering a Cake

Tim would like to order a cake.

Tim: Hi, I'd like to order a cake, please.

Clerk: Sure, for when?

Tim: This Saturday.

Clerk: Sure, which one?

Tim: The large rectangle one, please.

Clerk: What color would you like? We have white, blue, or pink.

Tim: Pink, please.

Clerk: Okay, what would you like written on it?

Tim: Happy Birthday Molly.

Clerk: Okay, we'll have that ready for pick-up by 10 am on Saturday.

Check your Understanding

1. Why is Tim buying a cake?

2. What shape is the cake?

3. Can Tim pick up the cake before, or after 10 am on Saturday?

Answers

1. He's buying a cake for Molly's birthday.

2. It's a rectangle.

3. He can pick up the cake after 10 am.

#89: Taking a Taxi

Jenny is taking a taxi to the airport.

Taxi driver: Where would you like to go?

Jenny: To the airport, please. Do you go there?

Taxi driver: Yes, I do.

Jenny: About how much will it cost?

Taxi driver: Around $50.

Jenny: Okay. Sounds good.

Taxi driver: You're going to departures?

Jenny: Yes, please.

Taxi driver: Domestic or international terminal?

Jenny: Domestic terminal, please.

Check your understanding

1. Is Jenny going to another country?
2. Does the taxi go to the airport?
3. Is Jenny picking someone up at the airport?

Answers

1. No, probably not.
2. Yes, it does.
3. No, she isn't.

#90: A Noisy Hotel Room

Tom would like to switch rooms at his hotel.

Tom: Hi, my room is loud! It was difficult to sleep last night.

Clerk: What was the problem?

Tom: The noise from the street. There was so much traffic.

Clerk: I'll check if there's a room on the other side of the building.

Tom: Thank you.

Clerk: Okay. We do have another room but only for tonight. Then, you'd have to switch again for your last night.

Tom: Oh? That's a big hassle. I'll stay where I am and buy some earplugs.

Check your Understanding

1. Why doesn't Tom like his hotel room?
2. Is Tom going to change rooms? Why or why not?
3. What's Tom's solution?

Answers

1. It's too noisy.
2. No, he isn't. He'd have to switch twice.
3. He's going to buy earplugs.

#91: Making an Appointment

Tom is making an appointment with his doctor on the phone.

Tom: Can I make an appointment for tomorrow, please?

Jenny: Sure, with which doctor?

Tom: Dr. Brown.

Jenny: We have nothing tomorrow but how about Wednesday?

Tom: Sure, that's fine.

Jenny: Okay, I'll put you in for 2:00?

Tom: Sounds good.

Jenny: What are you coming in for?

Tom: I have a sore toe.

Jenny: Okay, we'll see you on Wednesday.

Check your Understanding

1. Why does Tom want to see his doctor?

2. When is he going to see the doctor?

3. What is his preferred appointment day?

Answers

1. He wants to see his doctor because he has a sore toe.

2. He will see his doctor on Wednesday at 2:00.

3. His preferred appointment day is tomorrow.

#92: Talking to the Doctor

Carrie is discussing her problem with the doctor.

Doctor: Hi Carrie, what can I help you with today?

Carrie: I've been having lots of stomachaches lately.

Doctor: I see. Have you changed your diet recently?

Carrie: No, just the usual.

Doctor: What about stress? Any big thing coming up?

Carrie: Yes, I just changed jobs. I'm having trouble sleeping too.

Doctor: Do you think that might be the cause of it?

Carrie: It could be. It's been very stressful learning all the new systems at work.

Doctor: Are you exercising and eating healthy foods?

Carrie: No, I don't have time.

Doctor: That might make a big difference.

Check your Understanding

1. Does the doctor suggest medicine?

2. What is likely causing the stomachaches?

3. What other problem does she have besides stomachaches?

Answers

1. No, the doctor suggests exercise and eating healthy foods.

2. It might be stress from a new job.

3. She's also having trouble sleeping.

#93: More Ketchup, Please

Tim would like some things from the waiter.

Tim: Excuse me, could I please get some more ketchup for my fries?

Waiter: Sure, no problem. I'll bring you the bottle.

Tim: Oh, and some hot sauce too.

Waiter: Okay.

Tim: Thank you! Sorry to be such a hassle.

Waiter: Oh, no problem at all.

Tim: Wait. I'd love more Coke. Do you have free refills?

Waiter: Yes, I'll get you another one. Anything else before I go?

Tim: No, I think that's it for now.

Check your Understanding

1. How many things does Tim need?

2. Does Tim have to pay for another Coke?

3. Why does Tim want more ketchup?

Answers

1. He needs three things: Coke, ketchup, and hot sauce.

2. No, there are free refills.

3. He wants more ketchup for his fries.

#94: No Mayo, Please

Tim's order is wrong at a restaurant.

Tim: Excuse me, I ordered my burger with no mayo. But, I think there's some on it. I hate mayo.

Waitress: The kitchen must have missed that. I had that on the order. Can I get you a new one?

Tim: Yes, please.

Waitress: No problem. It should be about 10 minutes.

Tim: Thank you.

Waitress: Sorry for getting that wrong.

Check your Understanding

1. What does Tim not like?
2. Did the waitress make a mistake?
3. How long will it take to make a new burger?

Answers

1. He doesn't like Mayo.
2. No, the people cooking the burger did.
3. It will take about 10 minutes.

#95: A Phone Problem

Tim needs help with his cellphone.

Repair person: What can I help you with?

Tim: My phone doesn't stay charged for long anymore.

Repair person: Okay, how long does the battery last?

Tim: Only a couple of hours usually.

Repair person: How old is the phone?

Tim: Six years now.

Repair person: Okay, well we could replace the battery but it's kind of expensive.

Tim: How much?

Repair person: It can be around $200. It might be worth considering a new phone. Other things will start to break soon if it's six years old.

Tim: Thanks for the advice. I'll get a new phone.

Check your Understanding

1. What's wrong with his phone?

2. Is Tim going to repair or replace his phone?

3. How old is the phone?

Answers

1. The battery dies very quickly.

2. He will replace his old phone.

3. It's six years old.

#96: Cancelling an Appointment

Tom would like to cancel his dentist appointment.

Tom: Hi, I'd like to cancel my appointment, please.

Clerk: Sure, what's the name?

Tom: Tom Waits.

Clerk: When is your appointment?

Tom: It's at 9 am tomorrow.

Clerk: Oh, we have a $50 cancellation fee for less than 24 hours. Would you still like to cancel?

Tom: Yes, please. I'll pay the fee.

Clerk: Okay, I got it. Would you like to reschedule?

Tom: No, thanks. That's okay.

Clerk: Okay, take care.

Check your Understanding

1. Why does Tom have to pay $50?

2. Does he want to reschedule?

3. Why does he want to cancel his appointment?

Answers

1. He has to pay $50 for cancelling within 24 hours.

2. No, he doesn't.

3. We don't know why he wants to cancel it.

#97: Ordering Sushi

Tim is ordering some sushi.

Tim: Hi, can I put in an order for 12:30, please?

Waiter: Sure, that's for pick-up?

Tim: Yes, please.

Waiter: What would you like?

Tim: 1 combo A and 1 vegetarian combo.

Waiter: Okay. Would you like miso soup with that?

Tim: Is it included?

Waiter: Yes.

Tim: Sure, I'll take two then.

Waiter: Okay, what's your name and phone number?

Tim: Tim. 778-385-2821.

Check your Understanding

1. Is Tim getting the sushi delivered?

2. What is Tim ordering?

3. Does he have to pay extra for the soup?

Answers

1. No, he's picking it up.

2. He's getting two combos and two miso soups.

3. No, he doesn't.

#98: Leaving a Message?

Tom wants to talk to Jim.

Tom: Hi, could I please talk to Jim?

Receptionist: Jim Ford?

Tom: Yes, please.

Receptionist: Okay, I'll put you through.

Tom: Thank you.

Receptionist: He's not answering. Would you like to leave a message?

Tom: Oh. Do you know when he'll be back?

Receptionist: He's probably on lunch right now. You could try again in an hour?

Tom: Sounds good. I'll do that.

Check your Understanding

1. Is Jim in the office now?

2. Does Tom want to leave a message?

3. Does the receptionist know where Jim is?

Answers

1. No, he's not.

2. No, he'll try calling back later.

3. He guesses that Jim is on lunch but he's not sure.

#99: Reporting an Accident

Jenny called 911 to report a car accident.

Operator: Hi, what's your emergency?

Jenny: I just saw a car accident happen.

Operator: Where are you?

Jenny: At the corner of Green and Oak Street.

Operator: How many cars?

Jenny: Four cars.

Operator: Okay, stay on the line. I have more questions. Police and ambulance are on their way. Does it look serious?

Jenny: Yes, two of the cars are totalled.

Operator: Are people getting out of their cars?

Jenny: Not the people in the two worst cars. I don't see them moving.

Check your Understanding

1. Is it a serious accident?

2. How many cars are involved?

3. Should Jenny hang up the phone?

Answers

1. Yes, it is.

2. There are four cars in the accident.

3. No, she should wait until the police or ambulance is there.

#100: A Hangover

Tom isn't feeling well because he had too much to drink.

Jenny: I'm bored! Let's go watch a movie.

Tom: Hey Jenny, I'm not feeling well right now.

Jenny: Oh no, what's wrong?

Tom: I know it's my fault but I have a terrible hangover.

Jenny: Why do you always drink so much? I hope you at least had a fun night. Do you need anything?

Tom: Could you grab me some aspirin, please?

Jenny: Sure, I'll pick you up a bottle and stop by.

Check your Understanding

    1. Does Tom regularly drink too much?

    2. What is Jenny going to bring Tom?

    3. What does Jenny want to do?

Answers

    1. Yes, he does.

    2. She's going to bring him some aspirin.

    3. She wants to go to a movie with Tom.

#101: Refrigerator Problems

Tom is having problems with his fridge.

Tom: Hi, I'm having some problems with my fridge. Do you repair them?

Repair person: Yes, we do. What seems to be the problem?

Tom: It's not as cold as it used to be.

Repair person: How old is it?

Tom: Around 15 years I think.

Repair person: And what brand?

Tom: Samsung.

Repair person: Okay, we can send someone over. Is tomorrow okay for you?

Tom: Sure. Can you come in the afternoon?

Repair person: Yes, we'll be there at 1:00.

Check your Understanding

1. What's the problem with the fridge?

2. Is someone going to come fix it?

3. How old is the fridge?

Answers

1. It's not that cold.

2. Yes, someone will come to fix it tomorrow.

3. It's 15 years old.

#102: A Missing Package

Sarah is trying to track down a missing package.

Sarah: Hi, it says that my package was delivered this afternoon but I don't see it. I got a text message saying that.

Delivery driver: Let me check. What's your tracking number?

Sarah: 103239082.

Delivery driver: Okay. It wasn't delivered to your house because you weren't home. You can find it at the post office down the street but only after 6:00. Do you see a delivery notice paper in your mailbox?

Sarah: Oh. There it is. I got it. Thanks for your help.

Delivery driver: Sure. You can pick it up today after 6:00.

Check Your Understanding

1. Why is Sarah calling?

2. Where is the package now?

3. Where can Sarah get her package after 6:00?

Answers

1. She's calling because she wants to know where her package is.

2. The package is probably on the delivery truck now. It will be at the post office at 6:00.

3. She can get the package at the post office.

Before You Go

If you found this book useful, please leave a review wherever you bought it. I'd really appreciate it.

Please send me an email with any questions or feedback.

YouTube: www.youtube.com/c/jackiebolen

Pinterest: www.pinterest.com/eslspeaking

ESL Speaking: www.eslspeaking.org

Email: jb.business.online@gmail.com

You might also be interested in these books (by Jackie Bolen):

- 1001 English Expressions and Phrases

- The Big Book of Phrasal Verbs in Use

- English Grammar Workbook for Beginners

Please join my email list. You'll get a helpful email, related to learning English delivered to your inbox every week: www.eslspeaking.org/learn-english.

Made in United States
Orlando, FL
26 December 2024